Ignite Your **Motivation** *for* **Success**

Gerard Assey

Ignite Your Motivation for Success

By

Gerard Assey

Published by:

Gerard Assey

19/18, Palli Arasan Street

Anna Nagar East

Chennai - 600 102

ISBN: 978-81-971121-6-4

(Image courtesy Freepik: www.Freepik.com-Thank You)

Table of Contents

Preface:
Igniting the Spark of Success

Welcome to a journey that transcends the pages of this book and invites you into the heart of motivation, resilience, and personal triumph. In these chapters, we embark on a exploration of the intricate dance between inspiration and achievement, a journey that traverses the realms of self-motivation, leadership dynamics, and the alchemy of team collaboration.
This book, **"Ignite your Motivation for Success"** is more than a collection of principles; it is a compass for those navigating the vast landscapes of personal and professional aspirations. The impetus behind this endeavor is rooted in the belief that within every individual lies the innate power to ignite the flames of motivation and chart a course towards enduring success.

The Genesis of Ignite:
The genesis of this book is woven into the stories of individuals who defied odds, transformed setbacks into stepping stones, and kindled the fires of motivation within themselves and those around them. It draws inspiration from the collective wisdom of leaders, visionaries, and ordinary individuals who, through unwavering determination, reshaped their destinies.

What Awaits You:
As you turn the pages, you will encounter chapters crafted with care, each dedicated to unraveling a facet of motivation. From understanding the essence of intrinsic drive to implementing leadership

strategies, fostering teamwork, and cultivating self-motivation, the narrative unfolds as a comprehensive guide for personal and collective growth.

But this book is not a monologue; it is an interactive exploration. Embedded within the chapters are practical action plans, real-world examples, and insightful anecdotes that bridge the gap between theory and application. It is an invitation to not only absorb principles but to actively apply them in the laboratory of your own life.

Why This Matters:

In a world that often presents challenges and uncertainties, the ability to harness motivation becomes a superpower. It is the force that propels us beyond limitations, fuels creativity, and transforms aspirations into achievements. Whether you are a leader seeking to inspire your team, an individual navigating personal goals, or someone simply looking for that spark to drive positive change, this book is crafted with you in mind.

A Personal Commitment:

I want to assure you that what you hold in your hands is not the output of an algorithm but a labor of love, created with a human touch. It draws from my understanding of the human experience, the nuances of motivation, and the stories that resonate across cultures and generations.

Your Journey Begins:

As you embark on this journey, consider it not just a book but a companion on your quest for personal and professional fulfillment. It is my sincere hope that the principles and insights within these pages become guiding lights, steering you toward a future illuminated by the brilliance of your own motivation.

With anticipation and excitement for the journey ahead,

Leveraging Every Little "Spark" of Motivation

In the grand tapestry of our lives, motivation often hides in the subtle corners, waiting to be uncovered. As we embark on this exploration of the motivational landscape, our first destination is the intimate realm of recognizing and leveraging every little spark of inspiration.

Consider the tale of Alex, a struggling artist with a passion for capturing the vibrancy of life on canvas. In the midst of life's challenges, he discovered that inspiration could be found in the simplest moments – a fleeting sunset, the laughter of children, or the aroma of fresh coffee. These seemingly insignificant sparks became the brushstrokes that painted his path to artistic acclaim.

It's in the ordinary, the mundane, and the everyday occurrences that we often discover the seeds of motivation. Whether it's the encouragement of a friend, the beauty of nature, or a small personal victory, these sparks, when recognized and harnessed, can ignite a powerful flame within us.

Throughout history, countless individuals have turned these sparks into roaring fires of achievement. Take the story of Marie Curie, who, despite facing adversity as a female scientist in the early 20th century, found motivation in her insatiable curiosity for the mysteries of the universe. Her relentless pursuit of knowledge, fueled by the smallest sparks of wonder, led to groundbreaking discoveries in the field of physics and chemistry.

In this chapter, we will explore the art of recognizing and appreciating these subtle motivators that surround us. We'll delve into the stories of everyday heroes who transformed their lives by paying attention to the whispers of inspiration. Their tales will serve as beacons, guiding us to appreciate the extraordinary potential within the seemingly ordinary. But recognizing these sparks is only the first step. We will journey together into the realm of harnessing these sparks, learning how to translate fleeting moments of motivation into sustained momentum. Picture Sarah, a corporate professional navigating the challenges of a demanding job. By acknowledging and actively cultivating the small sources of motivation in her daily routine, she transformed her work from a burden into a fulfilling journey of growth.

To bring these principles into tangible action, we present an actionable plan: the creation of a motivation journal. This simple yet profound tool will serve as your personal compass, guiding you to pinpoint the sparks that fuel your inner fire. Through daily reflections, you'll witness the gradual accumulation of motivation, transforming your journey one spark at a time.

As we embark further into this, remember that greatness often begins with a single spark. Open your heart and mind to the whispers of inspiration, and let us together uncover the extraordinary potential hidden within the ordinary moments of life.

Understanding Motivation

Motivation, that elusive force propelling us towards our goals, is both an art and a science, a delicate dance between desire and action. To truly harness its power, we must first embark on a journey to understand the intricate tapestry that is motivation.

At its core, motivation is the internal spark that drives individuals to initiate, sustain, and complete actions to achieve specific goals. It's the fuel that propels us beyond the inertia of the familiar towards the possibilities that lie ahead. To grasp the nuances of motivation, we must appreciate its various forms.

Defining Motivation: Motivation is not a one-size-fits-all concept. It manifests in diverse ways, adapting to the unique needs and aspirations of individuals. Imagine Maria, a student with a dream of becoming a doctor. Her motivation is woven with a desire to make a difference in people's lives, an intrinsic drive that fuels her late-night study sessions and propels her towards academic excellence.

Intrinsic and Extrinsic Motivation: Motivation takes on two primary forms: intrinsic and extrinsic. Intrinsic motivation stems from internal factors, where the sheer joy, passion, or personal satisfaction derived from an activity becomes the driving force. Take the example of Tom, a software developer, who spends weekends experimenting with new coding languages purely out of curiosity and the joy of creation.

On the other hand, extrinsic motivation is driven by external rewards or consequences. This could be the promise of a promotion at work, a bonus for meeting a target, or recognition from peers. While extrinsic motivation can be powerful in the short term, its effects may wane without a solid foundation of intrinsic motivation to sustain the journey.

The Evolution of Motivation: Motivation is a dynamic force, evolving over time and adapting to different contexts. Picture the early stages of a career, where the motivation to prove oneself and climb the professional ladder is often pronounced. As responsibilities and priorities shift, so does the nature of motivation. A seasoned executive may find motivation in mentoring and leaving a lasting impact on the next generation of leaders.

In different contexts, motivation wears different masks. The motivation that drives an artist to create a masterpiece may differ significantly from the motivation of an athlete pushing physical boundaries. Exploring these nuances helps us tailor our approach to motivation, recognizing that what inspires one person may not resonate with another.

As we unravel the layers of motivation, it becomes evident that this force is as unique as a fingerprint, shaped by our values, experiences, and aspirations. It's the intricate dance between intrinsic and extrinsic elements, the ever-changing rhythm of our journey, that makes motivation a captivating subject worthy of exploration.

To bring this understanding into actionable insights, consider reflecting on your own motivations. What internal sparks drive you? Are there external factors that provide additional impetus? By delving into the roots of your motivation, you lay the groundwork for a more nuanced and personalized approach to achieving your goals. As we journey further into the depths of motivation, let this understanding serve as a compass, guiding us towards a more profound connection with the force that propels us forward.

Empowering Ourselves and Others

In the symphony of life, motivation is not a solitary melody but a harmonious ensemble that resonates far beyond the individual. As we delve into the exploration of empowerment, we uncover the profound ripple effect that motivation has on both personal and collective success.

The Ripple Effect of Motivation: Consider the metaphorical pebble dropped into a pond. The ripples extend far beyond the point of impact, touching every shore in their path. Similarly, motivation possesses a ripple effect, shaping not only individual destinies but influencing the collective journey of communities, teams, and societies.

Think of Emma, an impassioned environmentalist. Her commitment to sustainability, driven by a deep-seated motivation to protect the planet, not only propels her towards eco-friendly practices but also inspires those around her. The ripple effect manifests as friends adopt recycling habits, colleagues engage in conservation initiatives, and a broader community rallies behind the cause.

As we navigate the waters of empowerment, it becomes evident that a motivated individual becomes a catalyst for positive change, setting off waves of inspiration that touch the lives of others. The interconnectedness of motivation illuminates its potential as a force capable of shaping a brighter and more empowered collective future.

Strategies for Motivating and Supporting Others: Empowerment extends beyond personal motivation; it involves uplifting those around us. This chapter explores strategies for not only igniting the flame within ourselves but also fanning the sparks of motivation in others.

Imagine a team leader, John, who understands the diverse sources of motivation within his team members. Some thrive on recognition, while others find motivation in collaborative problem-solving. John tailors his leadership approach, providing individualized support that fuels the motivation of each team member. This personalized strategy not only enhances individual performance but contributes to a collective synergy that propels the entire team towards success.

Empathy emerges as a cornerstone in empowering others. By understanding the unique motivations and challenges faced by individuals, we can offer targeted support. This may involve providing resources, acknowledging accomplishments, or simply being a compassionate listener.

Case Studies of Successful Leaders: To illuminate these principles, we delve into the stories of successful leaders who embody the art of empowerment. Consider the narrative of Michelle, a CEO renowned for fostering a culture of innovation within her organization. Her genuine passion for the company's mission and her ability to align individual aspirations with organizational goals create an environment where every employee feels motivated and valued.

Drawing inspiration from such leaders, we uncover actionable insights that can be applied in various contexts. Whether leading a team, managing a household, or contributing to a community initiative, the strategies employed by these leaders serve as guiding lights in our pursuit of collective empowerment.

As we immerse ourselves in the stories of these trailblazers, we find that true empowerment goes beyond individual success. It's about creating an ecosystem where each individual feels not only motivated but also equipped to contribute their unique talents to the collective journey.

To internalize these insights, consider developing a personalized action plan. Identify the motivators within your immediate circle, explore strategies to support their aspirations, and observe the transformative power of collective empowerment. Through this chapter, let us not only become architects of our own motivation but also ambassadors of inspiration, fostering a ripple effect that transcends boundaries and empowers the world around us.

Benefits of Being Highly Motivated and Repercussions of Not

In the grand tapestry of human experience, motivation is the invisible thread that weaves together the fabric of health, relationships, and career. As we journey through this chapter, we'll unfurl the profound impact of being highly motivated and, conversely, shine a light on the repercussions of lacking this essential force.

Illustrating the Positive Impact of Motivation:

- ✓ *Health:* Consider the story of Mark, who, motivated by a desire for a healthier lifestyle, embraced regular exercise and nutritious eating habits. The positive impact on his physical well-being transcended weight loss; it manifested in increased energy, improved sleep, and a heightened sense of overall well-being. Numerous studies corroborate these anecdotes, emphasizing the link between motivation, healthy habits, and a robust immune system.
- ✓ *Relationships:* Motivation serves as a silent architect of thriving relationships. Take the example of Lisa, who, motivated by a desire for deeper connections, invested time and effort in improving her communication skills. The ripple effect was profound – not only did her personal relationships flourish, but her strengthened interpersonal skills also elevated her professional collaborations. Motivated individuals often radiate positivity, fostering an

environment conducive to harmonious connections.

- ✓ *Career:* In the professional realm, the impact of motivation on career trajectory is undeniable. Picture Alex, motivated by a vision of career advancement. His proactive approach, fueled by a strong work ethic, not only earned him promotions but also positioned him as a leader within his organization. Motivation is the driving force behind innovation, resilience, and a relentless pursuit of excellence in the workplace.

Exploring the Consequences of Lacking Motivation:

- ✓ *Lack of Direction:* Conversely, the absence of motivation can cast a shadow on the path ahead. Without a guiding force, individuals may find themselves adrift, lacking a sense of purpose or direction. This lack of clarity can permeate various aspects of life, leading to indecision and a diminished sense of fulfillment.
- ✓ *Stagnation in Relationships:* In personal relationships, a lack of motivation may result in stagnation. Without the impetus to invest time and effort, relationships may plateau, and the initial vibrancy may fade. Communication may dwindle, and emotional connections may erode, contributing to a sense of disconnect.
- ✓ *Career Plateau:* Professionally, a dearth of motivation can translate into a stagnant career. Opportunities for growth may be overlooked, and complacency may set in. This not only hampers individual progress but also

impacts team dynamics and overall organizational success.

Action Plan: Conducting a Self-Assessment:
To navigate the intricacies of motivation, embark on a journey of self-discovery. Consider conducting a comprehensive self-assessment to gauge your current state of motivation. Reflect on your short-term and long-term goals, identifying the driving forces that propel you forward or potential areas lacking inspiration.
Create a personalized map that outlines your aspirations and the motivations behind them. Are there areas in your life where motivation is thriving, and others where it may need a gentle nudge? By taking stock of your motivational landscape, you lay the groundwork for targeted interventions, ensuring that the positive impact of motivation permeates every facet of your existence.

As we immerse ourselves in the duality of motivation – its benefits and the repercussions of its absence – let this chapter serve as a mirror reflecting the profound impact motivation has on the canvas of our lives. Through self-awareness and intentional action, we pave the way for a future where motivation becomes the driving force behind our health, relationships, and career success.

Conducting a Self-Assessment to Understand the Current State of Motivation: Action Plan

Step 1: Define Your Goals and Aspirations

- ✓ **Personal Goals:** Clearly articulate your short-term and long-term personal aspirations. These could include health and fitness objectives, personal development goals, or lifestyle changes.
- ✓ **Professional Goals:** Outline your career ambitions, including specific milestones you aim to achieve. Consider both short-term advancements and long-term career objectives.
- ✓ **Relationship Goals:** Reflect on your relationships, identifying areas where you seek improvement or growth. This could involve strengthening existing connections or fostering new ones.

Step 2: Identify Motivators and Sources of Inspiration

- ✓ **Intrinsic Motivators:** List internal factors that drive you, such as personal values, passions, and a sense of purpose. Reflect on activities or pursuits that bring you joy and fulfillment.
- ✓ **Extrinsic Motivators:** Identify external factors that influence your motivation, such as recognition, rewards, or achievements. Consider how external validation contributes to your sense of accomplishment.

Step 3: Assess Current Motivational Levels

- ✓ **Reflection Time:** Allocate dedicated time for introspection. This could be through journaling, meditation, or deep contemplation. Ask yourself probing questions about your current levels of motivation in various aspects of your life.
- ✓ **Feedback from Others:** Seek input from trusted friends, family members, or colleagues. They may provide valuable insights into your motivational patterns and offer perspectives that you might not have considered.

Step 4: Analyze Patterns and Trends

- ✓ **Patterns of Motivation:** Identify recurring themes or patterns in your sources of motivation. Explore whether certain activities consistently energize you or if there are consistent de-motivators.
- ✓ **Environmental Factors:** Consider how your physical and social environments influence your motivation. Evaluate whether your surroundings enhance or hinder your ability to stay motivated.

Step 5: Set SMART Goals Based on Assessment

- ✓ **Specific:** Clearly define your goals based on the insights gained from your self-assessment. Ensure they are specific and tailored to your unique motivations.
- ✓ **Measurable:** Establish criteria to measure progress. This could involve creating milestones or incorporating quantifiable metrics related to your goals.
- ✓ **Achievable:** Set goals that are challenging yet realistic. Consider your current

circumstances and the resources available to you.

- ✓ **Relevant:** Align your goals with your overarching life aspirations. Ensure they contribute to your sense of purpose and fulfillment.
- ✓ **Time-Bound:** Establish clear timelines for achieving your goals. This helps create a sense of urgency and structure to your action plan.

Step 6: Create a Motivation Journal

- ✓ **Daily Entries:** Commit to maintaining a motivation journal. Record daily reflections on moments of inspiration, achievements, and areas where motivation may be lacking.
- ✓ **Gratitude Entries:** Include aspects of your life that you are grateful for. Gratitude can serve as a powerful motivator by shifting your focus to positive elements.
- ✓ **Challenges and Solutions:** Document challenges you encounter and brainstorm potential solutions. This proactive approach helps you address obstacles and maintain motivation.

Step 7: Seek Accountability and Support

- ✓ **Accountability Partner:** Share your goals and action plan with a trusted friend, mentor, or family member. Having someone to hold you accountable can significantly impact your commitment.
- ✓ **Support System:** Surround yourself with individuals who inspire and support your journey. A positive and motivating social network can contribute to sustained motivation.

Step 8: Regularly Review and Adjust Your Action Plan

- ✓ **Scheduled Check-Ins:** Establish regular intervals for reviewing your progress. This could be weekly, monthly, or quarterly check-ins to assess your achievements and adjust your action plan accordingly.
- ✓ **Adaptability:** Be open to adjusting your goals and strategies based on changing circumstances or new insights. A flexible approach ensures your action plan remains aligned with your evolving needs.

By diligently following this comprehensive action plan, you embark on a journey of self-discovery and intentional growth. Through continuous self-assessment, goal-setting, and adaptation, you empower yourself to navigate the complex landscape of motivation, ensuring sustained progress towards a fulfilling and purpose-driven life.

Diagnosing and Building the Motivational Environment

In the theater of our lives, the stage we set significantly influences the narrative that unfolds. In this chapter, we venture into the art of diagnosing and building the motivational environment – a tapestry woven from the threads of our workplace, home, and social spaces. We'll explore the subtleties of atmosphere, address common obstacles that shroud motivation, and craft a personalized roadmap for cultivating an environment that nurtures inspiration.

Creating a Motivational Workplace, Home, and Social Atmosphere:

- ✓ *The Workplace:* Imagine Sarah, a professional thriving in an environment where collaboration is encouraged, achievements are celebrated, and the vision of the company aligns with her personal values. The workplace serves as a crucible for motivation when it fosters a sense of purpose, provides opportunities for growth, and values the well-being of its employees.
- ✓ *The Home:* Consider the home as a sanctuary where motivation is not only welcomed but also cultivated. A home environment that encourages open communication, supports personal aspirations, and provides a tranquil space for reflection becomes a catalyst for individual and collective motivation. The home serves as a foundation for emotional well-being, resilience, and personal growth.

- ✓ *Social Spaces:* Our social circles, whether friends, family, or community, play a pivotal role in shaping our motivational atmosphere. Positive, uplifting relationships contribute to a sense of belonging and provide encouragement during challenging times. A social environment that values collaboration over competition and celebrates individual achievements fosters a collective spirit of motivation.

Addressing Common Obstacles to Motivation:

- ✓ *Negative Influence:* Identify and mitigate negative influences in your environment. These could be individuals, media, or external factors that dampen motivation. Surround yourself with positivity and limit exposure to sources that breed negativity.
- ✓ *Lack of Clarity:* Ambiguity can stifle motivation. Clearly define your goals and aspirations in each environment – workplace, home, and social spaces. When the path ahead is well-lit, motivation finds a natural ally in clarity.
- ✓ *Unsupportive Structures:* Examine the structures within your environments. In the workplace, this could involve organizational policies or leadership styles. At home, it may entail the division of responsibilities and communication dynamics. Identify and address structures that hinder motivation, advocating for changes when necessary.

Action Plan: Develop a Personalized Motivational Environment Checklist:

- ✓ *Identify Motivational Triggers:* List elements in your environment that consistently inspire and energize you. These could be visual cues, supportive relationships, or specific activities. Use these triggers as foundational elements in your motivational environment.
- ✓ *Assess and Remove Obstacles:* Conduct a thorough assessment of each environment – workplace, home, and social spaces. Identify obstacles to motivation, both internal and external. Develop strategies to either remove or navigate these obstacles effectively.
- ✓ *Set Boundaries:* Establish clear boundaries to protect your motivational environment. This could involve setting limits on negativity, carving out dedicated spaces for focused work or relaxation, and communicating expectations in your social circles.
- ✓ *Incorporate Positive Rituals:* Introduce rituals that enhance motivation within each environment. This could be a morning routine that sets a positive tone for the day, a designated space for reflection and goal-setting, or regular social activities that foster a sense of connection.
- ✓ *Regularly Evaluate and Adjust:* Create a routine for evaluating the effectiveness of your motivational environment checklist. Regularly reassess your triggers, obstacles, and rituals, adjusting them as your goals and circumstances evolve.

Consider the example of James, who transformed his home office into a vibrant space adorned with motivational quotes, natural light, and greenery. By addressing common obstacles, setting clear boundaries, and incorporating positive rituals, James created an environment that not only bolstered his work productivity but also contributed to a heightened sense of well-being.

In the symphony of life, the environments we cultivate become the orchestrators of motivation. Through intentional design, proactive obstacle management, and the infusion of positivity, we pave the way for an atmosphere that not only supports our aspirations but propels us towards the zenith of inspiration. Let this chapter be your guide as you embark on the transformative journey of diagnosing and building the motivational environment that fuels your pursuit of success.

Developing a Personalized Motivational Environment Checklist-Action Plan

Step 1: Identify Motivational Triggers

Objective: Recognize elements in your environment that consistently inspire and energize you.

- ✓ **Reflective Analysis:** Spend time reflecting on moments or spaces where you've felt exceptionally motivated. Consider what aspects of the environment contributed to this motivation.
- ✓ **List Your Triggers:** Create a comprehensive list of these motivational triggers. They could be visual cues, specific people, activities, or even particular settings.
- ✓ **Prioritize Triggers:** Identify the triggers that have the most significant impact on your motivation. This will help you focus on incorporating them into your daily environments.

Step 2: Assess and Remove Obstacles

Objective: Conduct a thorough assessment of each environment, identifying and addressing obstacles to motivation.

- ✓ **Environmental Audit:** Evaluate your workplace, home, and social spaces. Identify any physical or structural aspects that hinder motivation, such as clutter, poor lighting, or disorganized spaces.
- ✓ **Internal Obstacles:** Reflect on personal obstacles, such as self-doubt, procrastination,

or negative thought patterns. Develop strategies to address these internal barriers.

- ✓ **Communication Channels:** Assess the communication dynamics within your environments. Ensure that there's clear and positive communication, reducing the risk of misunderstandings or conflicts that may hamper motivation.

Step 3: Set Boundaries

Objective: Establish clear boundaries to protect and enhance your motivational environment.

- ✓ **Negativity Management:** Define limits on exposure to negativity. This could involve reducing time spent on negative news or distancing yourself from individuals who consistently contribute to a negative atmosphere.
- ✓ **Designated Spaces:** Create dedicated spaces for specific activities. Establish a workspace conducive to focus and productivity, a relaxation area free from work-related stress, and social spaces designed for positive interactions.
- ✓ **Communication Expectations:** Clearly communicate your expectations regarding communication in both personal and professional settings. Establish boundaries to ensure that your time and energy are respected.

Step 4: Incorporate Positive Rituals

Objective: Introduce rituals that enhance motivation within each environment.

- ✓ **Morning Routine:** Develop a morning routine that sets a positive tone for the day. This could include activities like meditation, exercise, or gratitude journaling.

- ✓ **Workspace Rituals:** Incorporate rituals specific to your workspace. This might involve starting each work session with a motivational quote, setting clear daily goals, or organizing your workspace before beginning tasks.
- ✓ **Social Connection Rituals:** Foster positive social connections through rituals. This could be regular social activities, virtual or in-person, that contribute to a sense of community and support.

Step 5: Regularly Evaluate and Adjust

Objective: Create a routine for evaluating the effectiveness of your motivational environment checklist and make adjustments as needed.

- ✓ **Scheduled Reviews:** Establish regular intervals for reviewing the impact of your checklist. This could be weekly, monthly, or quarterly assessments.
- ✓ **Feedback Gathering:** Seek feedback from yourself and, if applicable, from others in your environment. Assess whether the checklist elements are contributing to a positive and motivating atmosphere.
- ✓ **Adaptation Strategies:** Be open to adjusting your checklist based on evolving goals, circumstances, or feedback. Flexibility is key to ensuring the ongoing effectiveness of your motivational environment.

Consider this example: Emily identified that natural light and greenery in her workspace were powerful motivators. She incorporated these elements, set boundaries around negativity, established a morning routine, and regularly evaluated her checklist. Over time, this transformed her workspace into a haven of productivity and inspiration.

By following this comprehensive action plan, you not only create a checklist tailored to your unique needs but also establish a dynamic process for continuous improvement. Your personalized motivational environment checklist becomes a living document, evolving with you on your journey toward sustained inspiration and success.

Basing Progress on Your Own Improvements

In the era of social media and perpetual connectivity, the allure of comparison beckons from every corner, casting a shadow on our personal journeys. As we traverse the landscape of progress, this chapter delves into the perilous danger of constant comparison, advocates for the celebration of personal milestones and growth, and crafts a thoughtful action plan to establish personal benchmarks for success.

The Danger of Constant Comparison:
In a world adorned with curated snapshots of success, the temptation to measure our progress against the perceived achievements of others is ever-present. Picture Alice, a budding entrepreneur, scrolling through social media platforms showcasing the triumphs of her peers. The danger lies not in admiration but in the tendency to internalize these comparisons, allowing them to morph into benchmarks that overshadow our unique journeys.
Constant comparison breeds discontent and undermines the significance of personal progress. It's a deceptive mirage, masking the trials and tribulations that shape each individual's story. The danger isn't merely in comparing apples to oranges, but in overlooking the orchard of personal growth that flourishes when we focus on our unique path.

Celebrating Personal Milestones and Growth:
Contrary to the allure of external benchmarks, genuine progress stems from within. Imagine John,

an artist committed to refining his craft. Instead of fixating on the accolades of others, John chooses to celebrate his personal milestones – the subtle improvements in technique, the courage to experiment with new styles, and the resilience to push through creative blocks.

Celebrating personal growth involves embracing the journey rather than fixating on the destination. It's about recognizing the small victories, appreciating the lessons learned in moments of adversity, and acknowledging the evolution that transpires with each step forward. The essence of success lies not in eclipsing others but in surpassing our former selves.

Action Plan: Establish Personal Benchmarks for Success:

✓ *Reflection on Personal Values:*

Clarify Your Values: Identify your core values, aspirations, and long-term objectives. What truly matters to you beyond external validations?

Define Success on Your Terms: Establish a personalized definition of success that aligns with your values. It could be centered around personal growth, fulfillment, or contributing to a greater cause.

✓ *Setting Realistic and Measurable Goals:*

Identify Personal Goals: Break down overarching aspirations into realistic and measurable short-term goals. These could be related to personal development, career milestones, or health and well-being.

Milestones, not Finish Lines: Shift the focus from end destinations to milestones. Celebrate the incremental progress achieved with each milestone, recognizing that success is a journey, not a singular destination.

- ✓ *Cultivating a Growth Mindset:* Embrace Challenges: Cultivate a growth mindset by viewing challenges as opportunities for learning and improvement. Understand that setbacks are part of the journey toward success.

  Feedback as a Compass: Embrace constructive feedback as a guiding force. Use it to refine your approach, enhance your skills, and propel yourself further on your unique path.
- ✓ *Gratitude and Positive Reinforcement:* Gratitude Journaling: Incorporate gratitude journaling into your routine. Regularly reflect on the aspects of your journey that you're grateful for, fostering a positive mindset.

  Celebrate Small Wins: Acknowledge and celebrate small victories. These could be moments of resilience, instances of personal growth, or accomplishments that align with your established benchmarks.

Illustrative Example: Consider Mary, an aspiring writer. Instead of constantly comparing herself to bestselling authors, Mary establishes personal benchmarks. She celebrates completing her first draft, mastering a new writing technique, and persisting through moments of self-doubt. This approach not only nurtures her creative spirit but also propels her forward on a path uniquely tailored to her aspirations.

In the tapestry of personal progress, let this chapter be a guide toward cultivating an environment that values authenticity over comparison. As you embark on the journey of establishing personal benchmarks, remember that success is not a uniform destination but a mosaic of individual triumphs. Celebrate your growth, honor your unique path, and let the benchmarks you set be the compass guiding you towards a fulfilling and purpose-driven life.

Establishing Personal Benchmarks for Success- Action Plan

Objective: Create a roadmap for success grounded in personal values, realistic goals, and a growth mindset.

Step 1: Reflection on Personal Values

Clarify Your Values:

- ✓ Self-Discovery: Engage in introspection to identify your core values, passions, and overarching life purpose. Consider what truly matters to you beyond external expectations.
- ✓ Define Success on Your Terms: Articulate a personalized definition of success that resonates with your values. Ask yourself: What does success look like to you, independent of societal norms or external validations?

Step 2: Setting Realistic and Measurable Goals

Identify Personal Goals:

- ✓ Break Down Aspirations: Take your long-term aspirations and break them down into realistic and measurable short-term goals. These goals can span personal development, career milestones, health, relationships, and any other relevant domains.
- ✓ Milestones, not Finish Lines: Shift your perspective from singular end goals to milestones along the way. Recognize that success is a journey with incremental progress. What are the key milestones you aim to achieve?

Step 3: Cultivating a Growth Mindset

Embrace Challenges:

- ✓ Shift to a Growth Mindset: View challenges not as roadblocks but as opportunities for learning and improvement. How can you reframe setbacks as stepping stones to success?
- ✓ Feedback as a Compass: Embrace constructive feedback as a valuable tool for growth. Use feedback to refine your approach, enhance your skills, and propel yourself forward. How can feedback guide your journey?

Step 4: Gratitude and Positive Reinforcement

Gratitude Journaling:

- ✓ Reflect on Gratitude: Integrate gratitude journaling into your routine. Regularly reflect on aspects of your life and journey that you are grateful for. How does gratitude contribute to a positive mindset?
- ✓ Celebrate Small Wins: Develop a habit of acknowledging and celebrating small victories. These could be moments of resilience, instances of personal growth, or achievements aligned with your established benchmarks. How can you celebrate your small wins?

Example: Meet David, an aspiring entrepreneur. His values include creativity, autonomy, and making a positive impact. David's goals include launching a creative startup and fostering a healthy work-life balance.

- ✓ Value-Driven Goal: Launch a startup that aligns with his creative passions and contributes to a positive societal impact.
- ✓ Measurable Milestone: Develop and prototype the first product within the next six months, integrating eco-friendly materials.

- ✓ Growth Mindset Approach: Embrace challenges such as learning new marketing strategies and obtaining customer feedback as opportunities for growth.
- ✓ Gratitude Integration: Regularly journal about the small wins, like successfully completing a prototype or receiving positive feedback from early testers.
- ✓ Review and Adaptation:
- ✓ Scheduled Check-Ins: Establish regular intervals for reviewing progress. This could be monthly or quarterly check-ins to assess achievements and adjust goals.
- ✓ Adaptability: Be open to adjusting your benchmarks based on changing circumstances, evolving goals, or newfound insights. Flexibility ensures your action plan remains aligned with your dynamic journey.

By diligently following this action plan, you craft a blueprint for success that is uniquely yours. Your personal benchmarks become guiding stars, illuminating the path toward a fulfilling and purpose-driven life. As you celebrate small wins, embrace challenges, and integrate gratitude, remember that success is not a destination but a mosaic of personal triumphs along your unique journey.

Seeking Clarity on What You Want

In the labyrinth of life, the quest for success is akin to navigating uncharted territories. At the heart of this journey lies the pivotal concept of seeking clarity on what you want. This chapter illuminates the profound importance of defining clear goals, explores techniques for clarifying both personal and professional objectives, and draws inspiration from real-life success stories that emerged from the crucible of goal clarity.

The Importance of Defining Clear Goals:
Imagine Sarah, a recent graduate embarking on her professional journey. She faces a crossroads – a myriad of potential paths spread before her. Without a compass of clear goals, Sarah risks wandering aimlessly, unsure of which direction aligns with her aspirations. The first step towards success is anchoring oneself with the beacon of clear goals.
Clarity on what you want is the North Star that guides your decisions, shapes your actions, and propels you towards meaningful accomplishments. It transforms nebulous ambitions into tangible objectives, providing a roadmap for the journey ahead. Without this clarity, the path forward becomes obscured, hindering progress and diminishing the chances of realizing one's true potential.

Techniques for Clarifying Personal and Professional Objectives:
Reflection on Values:

- ✓ Values Assessment: Undertake a comprehensive assessment of your values.

What principles and beliefs are non-negotiable in your life? Aligning goals with your values ensures a sense of purpose and fulfillment.

- ✓ Personal Vision Statement: Craft a personal vision statement that encapsulates your long-term aspirations. This statement serves as a guiding force, outlining the destination you wish to reach.

SMART Goal Setting:

- ✓ Specific and Measurable Goals: Break down overarching aspirations into specific and measurable goals. Whether personal or professional, these goals should be clear, quantifiable, and achievable.
- ✓ Attainable and Relevant Objectives: Ensure that your goals are realistic and aligned with your overarching vision. Goals that resonate with your values and contribute to your sense of purpose are more likely to drive success.

Visualization Techniques:

- ✓ Visualization Practices: Utilize visualization techniques to vividly imagine the attainment of your goals. Visualization enhances clarity by creating a mental blueprint, making the journey towards success more tangible.
- ✓ Mind Mapping: Employ mind mapping to visually organize your thoughts and ideas. This technique aids in clarifying the interconnectedness of your goals and their relevance to your broader objectives.

Real-Life Success Stories Resulting from Goal Clarity:

- ✓ *The Entrepreneurial Visionary:* Consider the story of Alex, an entrepreneur with a vision to revolutionize sustainable packaging. Through a meticulous process of clarifying his goals, aligning them with his values, and setting SMART objectives, Alex transformed his vision into a reality. His company not only succeeded in creating eco-friendly packaging solutions but also contributed to a paradigm shift in the industry.

- ✓ *The Personal Development Journey:* Reflect on the journey of Emma, an individual passionate about personal development. Through a values assessment and visualization practices, Emma clarified her goals for continuous learning and skill enhancement. This clarity propelled her towards pursuing advanced certifications, ultimately leading to a fulfilling career transformation.

Action Plan: Cultivating Clarity on What You Want:

- ✓ Values Assessment: Dedicate time to assess your core values. What principles guide your decisions and actions? Write them down and reflect on their significance.
- ✓ Craft a Personal Vision Statement: Envision your ideal future and distill it into a concise personal vision statement. This statement should encapsulate the overarching aspirations that drive your journey.
- ✓ SMART Goal Setting: Break down your long-term aspirations into specific, measurable, attainable, relevant, and time-bound goals. Create a roadmap that outlines the steps needed to achieve these goals.

- ✓ Visualization Techniques: Experiment with visualization practices. Take time to vividly imagine the attainment of your goals. Picture the journey, the challenges, and the ultimate success.
- ✓ Mind Mapping: Use mind mapping to visually organize your goals and their interconnectedness. This visual representation can serve as a dynamic tool for gaining clarity on your objectives.
- ✓ Inspirational Insight: Meet David, a professional athlete who, through the clarity of his goals, transformed setbacks into stepping stones. By aligning his training objectives with his values and employing visualization techniques, David not only overcame challenges but also emerged as a champion, inspiring others to pursue their aspirations with unwavering clarity.

In the symphony of success, clarity on what you want acts as the conductor, harmonizing the diverse elements of your life. As you embark on the journey of seeking this clarity, let the stories of Alex, Emma, and David be guiding lights, illuminating the transformative power that arises when goals are defined with precision and purpose. This chapter beckons you to chart a course towards success by unveiling the clarity within your aspirations.

Internalizing the Motivation

In the pursuit of lasting success, the journey transcends the surface allure of momentary motivation. This chapter delves into the profound concept of internalizing motivation—an art that involves cultivating a deep, intrinsic drive that fuels sustained efforts towards personal and professional accomplishments. We'll explore the significance of moving beyond superficial motivation, discuss strategies for developing an internal drive, and illuminate the transformative power of meditation and visualization techniques in this profound process.

Moving Beyond Surface-Level Motivation:
Imagine Karen, a professional embarking on a fitness journey fueled by the desire to achieve a superficial goal—the aesthetics of physical fitness. Despite initial enthusiasm, Karen found herself wavering when external pressures and societal expectations became dominant motivators. The lesson here is clear: surface-level motivation, often derived from external validation, is ephemeral and lacks the resilience needed for enduring success.

To internalize motivation is to venture beyond the surface, delving into the core of personal desires, values, and aspirations. It's a shift from seeking validation from others to seeking fulfillment from within—a transformation that positions motivation as an intrinsic force, resilient to external fluctuations.

Developing a Deep, Internal Drive for Success:
Clarify Your Why:

- ✓ Reflect on Your Purpose: Take time to reflect on your purpose—your deep-seated "why" that propels you forward. What is the underlying motivation driving your actions and aspirations?
- ✓ Align with Core Values: Ensure that your goals align with your core values. Internalized motivation flourishes when there is congruence between your aspirations and the principles that define you.

Embrace Intrinsic Rewards:

- ✓ Shift from External Validation: Challenge the allure of external validation. Cultivate a mindset that values intrinsic rewards—personal growth, fulfillment, and the alignment of actions with values.
- ✓ Celebrate Intrinsic Achievements: Acknowledge and celebrate achievements that resonate with your internal motivations. These could be moments of personal growth, acts of kindness, or progress towards your deeper aspirations.

Meditation and Visualization Techniques for Internalizing Motivation:

Meditation for Inner Alignment:

- ✓ Mindful Meditation Practices: Engage in mindful meditation practices to foster inner alignment. These practices can include focused breathing, body scans, or mindfulness techniques that cultivate awareness of the present moment.
- ✓ Connect with Inner Motivation: During meditation, reflect on your inner motivations and aspirations. Visualize your goals and

allow the emotions associated with achieving them to surface, reinforcing your internal drive.

Visualization for Goal Integration:

- ✓ Visualization Techniques: Incorporate visualization as a tool for internalizing motivation. Create mental images of yourself achieving your goals, experiencing the emotions associated with success, and navigating challenges with resilience.
- ✓ Regular Visualization Sessions: Establish a routine of regular visualization sessions. This consistent practice reinforces the neural pathways associated with your goals, strengthening the connection between your internal motivations and your daily actions.

Inspirational Insight:

Consider the journey of Michael, an entrepreneur with a vision to empower underprivileged communities through sustainable initiatives. Michael's surface-level motivation initially stemmed from the external recognition of his philanthropic efforts. However, as he delved deeper into his purpose, aligning his goals with his values, Michael cultivated an internal drive that transcended accolades. This intrinsic motivation became the driving force behind his unwavering commitment to social impact.

Action Plan: Cultivating Internalized Motivation:

- ✓ Reflect on Your Purpose: Set aside dedicated time for introspection. Reflect on your purpose and the deep-seated motivations that underpin your goals.
- ✓ Align Goals with Core Values: Evaluate your goals and ensure they align with your core

values. Identify any misalignments and make adjustments to bring your aspirations in harmony with your principles.

- ✓ Shift from External Validation: Challenge the reliance on external validation. Develop a mindset that values the intrinsic rewards associated with personal growth and alignment with your deeper aspirations.
- ✓ Mindful Meditation Practices: Integrate mindful meditation into your routine. Engage in practices that foster inner alignment and bring awareness to your internal motivations.
- ✓ Visualization Techniques: Incorporate visualization as a regular practice. Create vivid mental images of achieving your goals, experiencing the associated emotions, and navigating challenges with resilience.
- ✓ Celebrate Intrinsic Achievements: Acknowledge and celebrate achievements that align with your internal motivations. Foster a habit of recognizing and valuing personal growth, kindness, and progress towards your deeper aspirations.

In the tapestry of success, internalized motivation weaves a thread of resilience, purpose, and enduring fulfillment. As you embark on the journey to cultivate this intrinsic drive, let the stories of individuals like Michael inspire you to embrace the transformative power of internalized motivation. This chapter beckons you to delve into the depths of your aspirations, anchoring your journey in a wellspring of motivation that emanates from the core of who you are.

Motion Leads to Motivation

In the dynamic interplay between action and inspiration, this chapter explores the symbiotic relationship between motion and motivation. We delve into the art of breaking the cycle of inactivity, understand how taking small actions becomes the catalyst for sustained motivation, and craft an actionable plan to create a daily routine that propels you forward on the path to success.

Breaking the Cycle of Inactivity:
Consider the scenario of Alex, an aspiring writer facing the weight of a blank page. Staring at the vast expanse of emptiness, Alex feels the inertia of inactivity, the stifling sense of being immobilized by the sheer magnitude of the task. Breaking this cycle requires recognizing that inaction begets stagnation, and stagnation, in turn, erodes motivation.
Breaking the cycle of inactivity involves taking that initial step, no matter how small, to disrupt the grip of inertia. It is the acknowledgment that motion, even in its minutest form, becomes the precursor to motivation.

How Taking Small Actions Fuels Motivation:
Consider Emma, a fitness enthusiast who, in moments of low motivation, commits to the simplicity of a ten-minute workout. This seemingly insignificant action sparks a cascade of positive effects. The act of motion, irrespective of its scale, serves as a testament to the possibility of progress, triggering a surge of motivation that propels Emma to extend her workout and consistently engage in physical activity.

The key lies in understanding that the relationship between motion and motivation is not unidirectional. It's a reciprocal dance where the act of moving, regardless of its magnitude, fuels the internal engine of motivation. Small actions act as building blocks, constructing a foundation of momentum that, over time, becomes a driving force.

Action Plan: Create a Daily Routine that Encourages Forward Momentum:

Morning Rituals for Momentum:

- ✓ Set a Positive Tone: Begin your day with positive affirmations or reflections. Create a morning ritual that sets an optimistic tone, reinforcing the belief that each day is an opportunity for progress.
- ✓ Small, Consistent Actions: Incorporate small, manageable actions into your morning routine. These could include brief exercises, mindful moments, or tasks that contribute to a sense of accomplishment.

Micro-Goals Throughout the Day:

- ✓ Identify Micro-Goals: Break down your larger goals into micro-goals. These are bite-sized actions that can be accomplished within a short timeframe. The achievement of these micro-goals serves as stepping stones towards broader aspirations.
- ✓ Scheduled Breaks for Movement: Integrate scheduled breaks into your day for physical movement. Whether it's a short walk, stretching exercises, or brief moments of relaxation, these breaks infuse your routine with moments of motion.

Reflective Evening Practices:

- ✓ Daily Review: End your day with a brief review of your accomplishments. Acknowledge the small actions taken and recognize their contribution to forward momentum. This reflection cultivates a positive mindset and fuels motivation for the next day.
- ✓ Visualize Tomorrow's Success: Before concluding your day, visualize the successful completion of tasks planned for the next day. This visualization primes your mind for motivation, creating a positive anticipation for the day ahead.

Inspirational Insight:

Consider the story of Sarah, an entrepreneur facing the challenge of launching her own business. Instead of succumbing to the overwhelming inertia, Sarah committed to the daily routine of setting small goals, taking incremental actions, and reflecting on her progress. This routine not only propelled her business forward but also cultivated a mindset where motivation became a natural byproduct of consistent motion.

Real-world Example:

James Clear, author of "Atomic Habits," emphasizes the concept of "Two-Minute Rule." If a task takes less than two minutes to complete, do it immediately. This small action creates momentum and often leads to the accomplishment of more significant tasks.

In the rhythm of life, motion becomes the melody that orchestrates the symphony of motivation. As you embark on the journey of creating a daily routine that encourages forward momentum, let the stories of individuals like Sarah and insights from thought leaders like James Clear inspire your commitment to consistent, small actions. This chapter invites you to recognize the transformative power of motion in fueling the fires of motivation, one step at a time.

Creating a Daily Routine that Encourages Forward Momentum-Action Plan

Objective: Develop a daily routine that integrates small, consistent actions to cultivate forward momentum and sustain motivation.

Morning Rituals for Momentum:

Set a Positive Tone:

- ✓ Activity: Begin your day with positive affirmations or reflections.
- ✓ Rationale: Creating a positive mindset from the outset reinforces the belief that each day is an opportunity for progress.

Small, Consistent Actions:

- ✓ Activity: Incorporate small, manageable actions into your morning routine, such as brief exercises, mindfulness, or tasks that contribute to a sense of accomplishment.
- ✓ Rationale: These small actions set a proactive tone, fostering a mindset of achievement early in the day.

Micro-Goals throughout the Day:

Identify Micro-Goals:

- ✓ Activity: Break down larger goals into micro-goals, which are small, achievable actions.
- ✓ Rationale: Micro-goals serve as attainable milestones, building a sense of accomplishment and contributing to forward momentum.

Scheduled Breaks for Movement:

- ✓ Activity: Integrate scheduled breaks into your day for physical movement, such as a short walk, stretching exercises, or relaxation moments.

- ✓ Rationale: These breaks infuse your routine with moments of motion, combating sedentary habits and energizing your mindset.

Reflective Evening Practices:

Daily Review:

- ✓ Activity: End your day with a brief review of your accomplishments, acknowledging the small actions taken.
- ✓ Rationale: Reflecting on achievements cultivates a positive mindset and reinforces the connection between action and progress.

Visualize Tomorrow's Success:

- ✓ Activity: Before concluding your day, visualize the successful completion of tasks planned for the next day.
- ✓ Rationale: Visualization primes your mind for motivation, creating a positive anticipation for the day ahead.

Adjustable Components for Personalization:

Flexibility for Adaptation:

- ✓ Activity: Establish a degree of flexibility in your routine to accommodate unexpected events or changes.
- ✓ Rationale: Flexibility ensures that your routine remains adaptable, reducing stress and promoting a sense of control.

Regular Review and Adjustment:

- ✓ Activity: Regularly review your daily routine, assessing its effectiveness, and adjusting as needed.
- ✓ Rationale: A routine should evolve with your goals and circumstances, ensuring its continued relevance and impact.

Inspirational Insight:
Example: Imagine Mark, a student juggling academics and part-time work. Mark's morning ritual includes setting aside 10 minutes for goal visualization. Throughout the day, he identifies micro-goals, like completing a chapter of reading or spending 15 minutes on a project. Scheduled breaks involve short walks, and in the evening, Mark reviews his accomplishments. This routine has not only enhanced Mark's productivity but has also ignited a consistent sense of motivation.

As you embark on implementing this action plan, remember that the key lies in consistency and adaptability. By weaving these activities into your daily routine, you create a tapestry of momentum and motivation. Your daily actions become the brushstrokes that paint a canvas of progress, ultimately leading to the realization of your broader aspirations.

Finding the Why Behind Your Motivation

In the intricate tapestry of human motivation, the "why" stands as the vibrant thread that weaves purpose into aspirations. This chapter explores the profound power of a compelling "why" in achieving goals, unveils tools for uncovering and refining your motivation, and draws inspiration from real-life examples of individuals whose unwavering sense of purpose propelled them to remarkable heights.

The Power of a Compelling "Why" in Achieving Goals:

Consider the tale of Maria, an aspiring environmental advocate. At the surface level, her goal was to champion sustainable practices. However, beneath this objective lay a profound "why"—a personal connection to nature forged in her childhood. Maria's commitment wasn't merely to save the environment; it was an impassioned pursuit driven by a deep-seated belief that the planet deserved safeguarding for future generations.

This illustrates the transformative power of a compelling "why." It transcends the superficial and anchors aspirations in a meaningful context. A robust "why" becomes the driving force that fuels resilience in the face of challenges, sustains motivation through adversity, and transforms goals into a journey of purpose.

Tools for Uncovering and Refining Your Motivation:

Reflective Self-Inquiry:

- ✓ Journaling Your Values: Engage in reflective journaling to identify and articulate your core values. Ask yourself: What principles guide your decisions and actions?
- ✓ The Five Whys Technique: Utilize the "Five Whys" technique to delve into the layers of your motivations. Ask why you want to achieve a particular goal, and then repeat the question until you reach the root cause.

Vision Boarding and Visualization:

- ✓ Create a Vision Board: Develop a vision board that visually represents your goals, values, and the deeper motivations behind them. The act of curating images reinforces the emotional connection to your aspirations.
- ✓ Future Self Visualization: Envision your future self having achieved your goals. Visualizing the tangible outcomes and the emotions associated with success deepens your connection to your motivation.

Real-Life Examples of Individuals Driven by a Strong Sense of Purpose:

- ✓ *Elon Musk's Mission to Mars:* Consider Elon Musk, the visionary entrepreneur behind SpaceX. Beyond the commercial goals of space exploration, Musk's "why" is rooted in a profound belief in the multi-planetary survival of humanity. This purpose-driven motivation not only fuels innovation but also galvanizes a collective sense of purpose among his team.
- ✓ *Malala Yousafzai's Advocacy for Education:* Reflect on Malala Yousafzai, the Nobel laureate and advocate for girls' education. Her "why" is deeply personal—an unwavering

commitment to the right to education, forged in the face of adversity. Malala's motivation extends beyond personal success; it is a commitment to a larger cause.

Action Plan: Uncover and Refine Your Motivation:

Reflective Journaling:

- ✓ Activity: Set aside dedicated time for reflective journaling. Explore your values, aspirations, and the emotions associated with your goals.

The Five Whys Technique:

- ✓ Activity: Apply the Five Whys technique to one of your goals. Start with the goal, then ask "why" repeatedly to uncover deeper motivations.

Create a Vision Board:

- ✓ Activity: Curate a vision board that visually represents your goals, values, and the deeper motivations behind them. Use images, quotes, and symbols that resonate with your sense of purpose.

Future Self Visualization:

- ✓ Activity: Set aside time for future self visualization. Envision your future self having achieved your goals, focusing on the emotions, experiences, and outcomes associated with success.

Inspirational Insight:

Example: Meet John, an aspiring entrepreneur. His initial goal was to build a successful business, driven by a desire for financial independence. Through reflective journaling, John discovered that his deeper motivation was rooted in a childhood dream of creating opportunities for others. This profound realization transformed his entrepreneurial journey into a purpose-driven pursuit of empowerment.

As you embark on the journey of uncovering and refining your motivation, let the stories of Elon Musk, Malala Yousafzai, and individuals like John inspire your exploration. Your "why" is the compass that guides your journey, and by cultivating a deep understanding of it, you infuse your goals with a sense of purpose that transcends the ordinary. This chapter beckons you to delve into the depths of your aspirations, unveiling the motivating forces that elevate your journey from mere achievement to meaningful fulfillment.

Tools for Uncovering and Refining Your Motivation

1. Reflective Self-Inquiry:
   - ✓ *Activity:* Engage in reflective journaling to identify and articulate your core values. Ask yourself: What principles guide your decisions and actions?
   - ✓ *Rationale:* Journaling provides a structured space for self-exploration, allowing you to delve into your beliefs, experiences, and aspirations.

Example:

- ✓ Prompt 1: What values are most important to me in life?
- ✓ Reflective Entry: Family, creativity, and making a positive impact on the environment are fundamental to my sense of purpose.
- ✓ *Activity:* Utilize the "Five Whys" technique to delve into the layers of your motivations. Ask why you want to achieve a particular goal, and then repeat the question until you reach the root cause.
- ✓ *Rationale:* The Five Whys technique is a structured approach to uncover the underlying motivations behind your goals, revealing deeper layers of purpose.

Example:

Goal: Start a fitness routine.

- ✓ Why 1: Why do I want to start a fitness routine? To improve my physical health.
- ✓ Why 2: Why is improving my physical health important? To have more energy and feel confident.

- ✓ Why 3: Why is having more energy and feeling confident important? To lead an active and fulfilling life.

2. Vision Boarding and Visualization:
   - ✓ *Activity:* Develop a vision board that visually represents your goals, values, and the deeper motivations behind them. Use images, quotes, and symbols that resonate with your sense of purpose.
   - ✓ *Rationale:* Vision boards provide a tangible representation of your aspirations, enhancing the emotional connection to your goals.

Example:

- ✓ Components: Images of a healthy lifestyle, quotes about perseverance, symbols representing personal growth.
- ✓ *Activity:* Set aside time for future self-visualization. Envision your future self having achieved your goals, focusing on the emotions, experiences, and outcomes associated with success.
- ✓ *Rationale:* Future self-visualization creates a vivid mental image that reinforces your connection to the positive emotions and achievements linked to your goals.

Example:

- ✓ Visualization: Imagine waking up energized and confident, engaging in activities you love, and feeling a profound sense of accomplishment.

Action Plan: Uncover and Refine Your Motivation

- ✓ Reflective Journaling:
- ✓ Set aside 15-20 minutes each day for reflective journaling.

- ✓ Use prompts such as values, aspirations, and emotional connections to guide your entries.

The Five Whys Technique:

- ✓ Choose a specific goal or aspiration.
- ✓ Ask "why" five times, noting each answer to uncover deeper motivations.
- ✓ Create a Vision Board:
- ✓ Gather materials like magazines, images, and quotes.
- ✓ Spend a dedicated time creating a visually compelling representation of your goals and motivations.

Future Self Visualization:

- ✓ Set aside 10-15 minutes for future self-visualization.
- ✓ Focus on the emotions, experiences, and outcomes associated with achieving your goals.
- ✓ Review and Adaptation:

Scheduled Reflections:

- ✓ Establish weekly or bi-weekly reflections to review your journal entries, Five Whys responses, and vision board.
- ✓ Adjustments:
- ✓ Be open to adjusting your tools based on what resonates most with you.
- ✓ If a particular tool proves especially effective, consider incorporating it more frequently into your routine.

By consistently engaging in these tools, you embark on a journey of self-discovery, uncovering the layers of your motivations and refining your sense of purpose. As you navigate this process, remember that self-awareness is a dynamic and evolving exploration, and each tool contributes to the intricate map of your motivations.

Helping You See That it's Worth the Effort

In the labyrinth of personal growth and achievement, this chapter illuminates the vital task of overcoming self-doubt and cultivating confidence. We delve into the transformative power of visualizing success and positive outcomes and provide a practical action plan for developing a self-affirmation routine. Through stories, examples, and actionable insights, we unravel the layers that shield your self-worth, guiding you toward the realization that the effort you invest is undeniably worth it.

Overcoming Self-Doubt and Building Confidence: Consider the story of Emily, a talented artist paralyzed by self-doubt. Despite receiving praise for her work, an internal narrative of uncertainty clouded her potential. Overcoming self-doubt requires a deliberate confrontation with these inner barriers. Confidence is not an innate trait; it's a skill cultivated through self-awareness, positive reinforcement, and a commitment to challenging one's own limiting beliefs.

Strategies for Overcoming Self-Doubt:

- ✓ Self-Reflection: Dedicate time to reflect on the origin of your self-doubt. What narratives or experiences have contributed to these doubts?
- ✓ Positive Affirmations: Counter negative thoughts with positive affirmations. Replace self-critical statements with empowering declarations about your abilities and worth.

- ✓ Skills Development: Invest in developing the skills relevant to your goals. Competence breeds confidence, and each improvement becomes a testament to your capabilities.

Visualizing Success and Positive Outcomes:
Visualization is a powerful tool that transcends mere imagination. It involves vividly picturing yourself achieving your goals, feeling the emotions associated with success, and visualizing positive outcomes. This mental rehearsal not only strengthens the neural pathways associated with success but also serves as a psychological anchor, fortifying your belief that your efforts will yield positive results.

Practical Techniques for Visualization:

- ✓ Create a Mental Movie: Imagine your journey towards success as a vivid mental movie. Picture the challenges, triumphs, and the ultimate realization of your goals.
- ✓ Sensory Visualization: Engage your senses in the visualization process. Feel the textures, hear the sounds, and immerse yourself in the sensory details of your envisioned success.
- ✓ Scripted Visualization: Write a detailed script of your success story. Describe the steps you take, the obstacles you overcome, and the emotions you experience along the way.

Action Plan: Develop a Self-Affirmation Routine:

- ✓ Identify Affirmation Themes:
  Reflect on the areas of your life where self-doubt is prevalent.

Identify affirmation themes that counteract these doubts, such as competence, resilience, or worthiness.

- ✓ Craft Positive Affirmations:
  Formulate positive affirmations that align with your identified themes.
  Ensure affirmations are concise, specific, and phrased in the present tense.
- ✓ Integration into Daily Routine:
  Incorporate affirmations into your daily routine. This could be during morning rituals, before significant tasks, or as part of bedtime reflections.
- ✓ Affirmation Reinforcement:
  Regularly revisit and revise your affirmations to reflect evolving goals and challenges.
  Use moments of self-doubt as cues to reinforce positive affirmations.

Inspirational Insight:
Consider the journey of Marcus, a budding entrepreneur. Struggling with self-doubt, he integrated positive affirmations into his routine, affirming his resilience, adaptability, and capacity for growth. Over time, these affirmations became a shield against doubt, paving the way for Marcus to confidently navigate challenges and build a successful venture.

Real-world Example:
Oprah Winfrey, despite her extraordinary success, openly shares her struggles with self-doubt. Through consistent self-affirmation and visualization, Oprah cultivated the unwavering belief that her efforts were worth the investment, ultimately realizing a level of success beyond her initial dreams.

Conclusion:

As you navigate the intricate terrain of self-worth and effort, let the stories of Emily, Marcus, and icons like Oprah illuminate the transformative potential within. This chapter beckons you to challenge the narratives of doubt, visualize the grand tapestry of success, and engrain positive affirmations into the fabric of your daily life. By developing the conviction that your efforts are undeniably worth it, you lay the foundation for a journey that transcends perceived limitations, unveiling the true worth of your endeavors.

Developing a Self-Affirmation Routine-Action Plan

Objective: Cultivate a consistent self-affirmation routine to overcome self-doubt, build confidence, and reinforce positive beliefs in your abilities and worth.

1. Identify Affirmation Themes:

- ✓ *Activity:* Reflect on the areas of your life where self-doubt is prevalent. Identify affirmation themes that counteract these doubts, such as competence, resilience, or worthiness.
- ✓ *Rationale:* Understanding the specific areas of self-doubt allows you to tailor affirmations to address these concerns directly.

Example:

Theme 1: Competence

- ✓ *Affirmation:* "I am capable and skilled in handling any challenges that come my way."

Theme 2: Resilience

- ✓ *Affirmation:* "I bounce back from setbacks stronger and more determined than ever."

2. Craft Positive Affirmations:

- ✓ *Activity:* Formulate positive affirmations that align with your identified themes. Ensure affirmations are concise, specific, and phrased in the present tense.
- ✓ *Rationale:* Well-crafted affirmations are powerful tools for reshaping your mindset and reinforcing positive beliefs.

Example:

- ✓ Affirmation 1: "I am a capable and resourceful problem solver."

- ✓ Affirmation 2: "My resilience empowers me to overcome challenges with grace and strength."

3. Integration into Daily Routine:

- ✓ *Activity:* Incorporate affirmations into your daily routine. This could be during morning rituals, before significant tasks, or as part of bedtime reflections.
- ✓ *Rationale:* Regular integration ensures that affirmations become a natural and consistent part of your thought process.

Example:

- ✓ Morning Ritual: Repeat affirmations while getting ready for the day.
- ✓ Before Tasks: Affirm before starting a challenging project.
- ✓ Bedtime Reflection: End the day by reinforcing positive beliefs about yourself.

4. Affirmation Reinforcement:

- ✓ *Activity:* Regularly revisit and revise your affirmations to reflect evolving goals and challenges. Use moments of self-doubt as cues to reinforce positive affirmations.
- ✓ *Rationale:* Adaptability and evolution ensure that your affirmations remain relevant and impactful over time.

Example:

- ✓ Monthly Review: Reflect on the effectiveness of your affirmations and adjust as needed.
- ✓ Challenge Response: When faced with self-doubt, consciously repeat affirmations to counteract negative thoughts.

Inspirational Insight:

Example: Imagine Sarah, a professional navigating a competitive industry. Her affirmation theme is

"Confidence." Her tailored affirmation is, "I exude confidence in my abilities and am deserving of success." Sarah integrates this affirmation into her routine, especially before client meetings. Over time, she notices a significant boost in her self-assurance and performance.

By consistently applying this action plan, you embark on a journey of self-empowerment. The affirmations become more than mere statements; they evolve into catalysts for positive change, reshaping your self-perception and fortifying your belief that your efforts are undeniably worth it. As you walk this path, remember that the commitment to affirming your worth is a profound investment in the most important journey of all—your personal growth and fulfillment.

Turning Rejection into Motivation

In the intricate dance of ambition, setbacks and rejections often cast shadows on the path to success. This chapter illuminates the art of resilience in the face of rejection, drawing inspiration from famous examples of individuals who transformed rejection into a stepping stone. We delve into the psychology of handling rejection and provide a practical action plan to develop a positive response strategy, turning rejection into a potent source of motivation.

Resilience in the Face of Setbacks:
Consider the journey of Michael Jordan, widely regarded as one of the greatest basketball players of all time. In high school, he faced rejection from the varsity team. Instead of succumbing to defeat, Jordan used this setback as fuel for his relentless work ethic, eventually leading him to multiple NBA championships and global acclaim.

Strategies for Resilience:

- ✓ Mindset Shift: Cultivate a growth mindset that views setbacks as opportunities for learning and improvement.
- ✓ Self-Reflection: Analyze the rejection objectively. Identify areas for growth without internalizing the rejection as a reflection of your worth.
- ✓ Adaptive Planning: Adjust your approach and goals based on the lessons learned from rejection. Flexibility is a hallmark of resilience.

Famous Examples of Individuals Using Rejection as a Stepping Stone:

- ✓ *J.K. Rowling:* The iconic author of the Harry Potter series faced numerous rejections before finding a publisher. She turned rejection into a driving force, using it as motivation to refine her work. Today, Rowling's books have sold millions of copies worldwide.
- ✓ *Colonel Sanders (KFC):* Harland Sanders, the founder of Kentucky Fried Chicken (KFC), faced rejection from over a thousand restaurants before finding one willing to franchise his recipe. His perseverance turned a series of rejections into a global fast-food empire.

Action Plan: Develop a Positive Response Strategy for Handling Rejection:

Initial Emotional Processing:

- ✓ *Activity:* Allow yourself a brief period to process and acknowledge the emotions associated with rejection.
- ✓ *Rationale:* This step prevents the suppression of emotions, fostering a healthy emotional release.

Objective Analysis:

- ✓ *Activity:* Objectively analyze the rejection. What specific aspects can you learn from?
- ✓ *Rationale:* An unbiased evaluation transforms rejection into constructive feedback.

Identify Growth Opportunities:

- ✓ *Activity:* Identify areas for personal or professional growth highlighted by the rejection.

- ✓ *Rationale:* Turning rejection into an opportunity for improvement shifts the narrative from failure to growth.

Adapt Goals and Strategies:

- ✓ *Activity:* Adjust your goals and strategies based on the insights gained from rejection.
- ✓ *Rationale:* Adaptive planning ensures that setbacks become stepping stones toward future success.

Cultivate a Positive Narrative:

- ✓ *Activity:* Reframe the rejection in a positive light. Emphasize the potential for future success.
- ✓ *Rationale:* Shifting your narrative cultivates resilience and maintains a forward-focused mindset.

Inspirational Insight:

Consider the story of Vera Wang, a renowned fashion designer. Initially rejected for the position of editor at Vogue, Wang embraced the setback. She redirected her career, eventually becoming one of the most influential figures in the fashion industry. Her rejection served as the catalyst for an extraordinary career in design.

Real-world Example:

Steve Jobs, after being ousted from Apple, the company he co-founded, used this rejection as a chance for introspection and innovation. He went on to establish NeXT and Pixar, ultimately returning to Apple and revolutionizing the tech industry.

As you navigate the inevitable landscape of rejection, remember that setbacks are not roadblocks but pivotal turns in your journey. The tales of Michael Jordan, J.K. Rowling, Colonel Sanders, Vera Wang, and Steve Jobs remind us that rejection can be a catalyst for unparalleled success. This chapter invites you to embrace rejection not as a deterrent, but as a powerful source of motivation, propelling you to heights beyond the reach of initial setbacks. Through resilience, analysis, and adaptive planning, you transform rejection into a cornerstone of your path to enduring success.

Developing a Positive Response Strategy for Handling Rejection-Action Plan

Objective: Cultivate a proactive and positive approach to handling rejection, transforming setbacks into opportunities for growth and motivation.

1. Initial Emotional Processing:

Activity: Allow yourself a brief period to process and acknowledge the emotions associated with rejection.

Rationale: Acknowledging and processing emotions prevents bottling up feelings, fostering a healthy emotional release.

Example:

Situation: Rejection from a job application.

Activity: Take a day to acknowledge and feel the disappointment. Allow yourself to experience the emotions without judgment.

2. Objective Analysis:

Activity: Objectively analyze the rejection. What specific aspects can you learn from?

Rationale: An unbiased evaluation transforms rejection into constructive feedback.

Example:

Situation: Manuscript rejection from a publisher.

Activity: Analyze the rejection letter for specific feedback. Identify areas that can be strengthened in future submissions.

3. Identify Growth Opportunities:

Activity: Identify areas for personal or professional growth highlighted by the rejection.

Rationale: Turning rejection into an opportunity for improvement shifts the narrative from failure to growth.

Example:

Situation: Rejection from a business pitch.

Activity: Identify specific skills or aspects of the pitch that can be improved. Consider seeking additional training or mentorship in those areas.

4. Adapt Goals and Strategies:

Activity: Adjust your goals and strategies based on the insights gained from rejection.

Rationale: Adaptive planning ensures that setbacks become stepping stones toward future success.

Example:

Situation: Rejection from a project proposal.

Activity: Reevaluate the project's goals and strategies. Consider incorporating feedback into a revised proposal, aligning it more closely with the needs of the stakeholders.

5. Cultivate a Positive Narrative:

Activity: Reframe the rejection in a positive light. Emphasize the potential for future success.

Rationale: Shifting your narrative cultivates resilience and maintains a forward-focused mindset.

Example:

Situation: Rejection from a scholarship application.

Activity: Reframe the rejection as an opportunity to explore alternative funding sources.

Focus on the potential for personal and academic growth through different avenues.

Inspirational Insight:

Example: Consider the journey of Thomas Edison, who faced countless failures while inventing the light bulb. His positive response strategy involved viewing each failure as a discovery of what didn't work, bringing him closer to success.

Real-world Example:

J.K. Rowling, after facing multiple rejections for her Harry Potter manuscript, embraced a positive response strategy. She used rejection as a motivator to refine her work, eventually finding success and becoming one of the most celebrated authors globally.

Conclusion:

This action plan is not a one-size-fits-all solution but a guide to developing a personalized strategy for handling rejection positively. By incorporating emotional processing, objective analysis, growth identification, adaptive planning, and cultivating a positive narrative, you transform rejection into a springboard for personal and professional advancement. Remember, the journey from rejection to success is a dynamic process, and each step you take contributes to the resilient narrative of your own success story.

Making Motivation Last

In the marathon of personal and professional pursuits, the ability to sustain motivation over the long term becomes a defining factor for success. This chapter unravels the strategies for nurturing enduring motivation, explores techniques to combat burnout, and provides a detailed action plan for establishing a maintenance routine to keep the flame of motivation burning brightly.

Strategies for Sustaining Long-Term Motivation:
Enduring motivation is not a fleeting spark but a sustained flame that withstands the winds of challenges. Consider the story of Marie Curie, the pioneering physicist and chemist. Motivated by a deep passion for scientific discovery, Curie's enduring commitment led to groundbreaking work in radioactivity. Her strategy for sustained motivation involved a harmonious blend of intrinsic curiosity and a relentless pursuit of knowledge.

Strategies for Long-Term Motivation:

- ✓ Intrinsic Connection: Align your goals with your core values and passions, fostering an intrinsic connection that sustains motivation through ups and downs.
- ✓ Progressive Goal Setting: Break down long-term goals into manageable milestones, celebrating each achievement along the way. The sense of progress fuels sustained motivation.
- ✓ Adaptability: Embrace change and adapt your goals to evolving circumstances. A flexible

approach prevents stagnation and maintains a sense of purpose.

Combating Burnout and Staying Inspired:

The shadow of burnout can dim even the brightest motivations. To combat burnout and stay inspired, it's crucial to cultivate a holistic approach that nourishes both mind and body. Oprah Winfrey's journey provides insights into overcoming burnout. Through practices like mindfulness, self-care, and a commitment to balance, Winfrey has sustained a remarkable career while staying true to her purpose.

Strategies for Combating Burnout:

- ✓ Mindfulness and Reflection: Incorporate regular mindfulness practices and reflection into your routine to maintain self-awareness and prevent burnout.
- ✓ Wellness Practices: Prioritize physical and mental well-being through regular exercise, adequate sleep, and healthy nutrition. A nourished body supports a resilient mind.
- ✓ Work-Life Integration: Seek a harmonious integration of work and personal life, avoiding excessive demands in any one area. Balance becomes a safeguard against burnout.

Action Plan: Establish a Maintenance Routine for Ongoing Motivation:

Intrinsic Connection Check:

- ✓ Activity: Regularly reflect on the intrinsic connection between your goals and core values.
- ✓ Rationale: Ensuring alignment with your values sustains motivation at its roots.

Progressive Goal Setting Session:

- ✓ Activity: Conduct a quarterly review of your long-term goals. Break them down into smaller milestones for the upcoming months.
- ✓ Rationale: Progressive goal setting maintains a sense of achievement and prevents stagnation.

Adaptability Exercise:

- ✓ Activity: Identify one aspect of your goals or plans that might need adjustment based on current circumstances.
- ✓ Rationale: Flexibility ensures continued relevance and prevents frustration.

Mindfulness Practice:

- ✓ *Activity:* Dedicate 10-15 minutes daily to mindfulness practices, such as meditation or deep breathing exercises.
- ✓ *Rationale:* Mindfulness enhances self-awareness and resilience, countering the effects of burnout.

Wellness Check-in:

- ✓ *Activity:* Schedule regular wellness check-ins to assess your physical and mental well-being.
- ✓ *Rationale:* Prioritizing health ensures sustained energy and motivation.

Work-Life Integration Audit:

- ✓ *Activity:* Assess the integration of work and personal life. Identify areas that may need adjustment for better balance.
- ✓ *Rationale:* A balanced life prevents burnout and maintains a holistic approach to motivation.

Inspirational Insight:

Example: The life of Nelson Mandela is a testament to enduring motivation. Through 27 years of imprisonment, Mandela maintained his commitment to the anti-apartheid cause. His resilience and unwavering dedication to justice showcase the power of motivation in the face of adversity.

Real-world Example:

Elon Musk's sustained motivation in the face of challenges with SpaceX and Tesla demonstrates the importance of adaptability. Musk's ability to adapt goals and strategies has been a key factor in his continued success.

As you embark on the journey of making motivation last, remember that it's not only about igniting the spark but also about nurturing a flame that withstands the tests of time. The stories of Marie Curie, Oprah Winfrey, Nelson Mandela, and Elon Musk illuminate the diverse paths to enduring motivation. This chapter invites you to weave these strategies into your daily life, creating a maintenance routine that becomes the bedrock of your sustained motivation—an enduring force that propels you toward lasting success.

Establishing a Maintenance Routine for Ongoing Motivation-Action Plan

Objective: Develop a personalized maintenance routine to sustain long-term motivation, combat burnout, and foster a resilient mindset.

1. Intrinsic Connection Check:

Activity: Regularly reflect on the intrinsic connection between your goals and core values.

Rationale: Ensuring alignment with your values sustains motivation at its roots.

Example:

Frequency: Weekly introspection.

Reflective Question: "How does my current pursuit align with my core values?"

Outcome: Reaffirmation of intrinsic connection or identification of areas needing adjustment.

2. Progressive Goal Setting Session:

Activity: Conduct a quarterly review of your long-term goals. Break them down into smaller milestones for the upcoming months.

Rationale: Progressive goal setting maintains a sense of achievement and prevents stagnation.

Example:

Frequency: Quarterly planning sessions.

Steps:

Review long-term goals.

Break goals into quarterly milestones.

Set specific, measurable targets.

Outcome: A detailed roadmap with achievable milestones.

3. Adaptability Exercise:

Activity: Identify one aspect of your goals or plans that might need adjustment based on current circumstances.
Rationale: Flexibility ensures continued relevance and prevents frustration.
Example:
Frequency: Monthly adaptability check.
Steps:
Assess current circumstances.
Identify potential adjustments to goals.
Outcome: Increased adaptability and resilience to changing conditions.

4. Mindfulness Practice:

Activity: Dedicate 10-15 minutes daily to mindfulness practices, such as meditation or deep breathing exercises.
Rationale: Mindfulness enhances self-awareness and resilience, countering the effects of burnout.
Example:
Practice: Mindful breathing.
Setting: Quiet space in the morning.
Outcome: Improved focus, reduced stress, and enhanced emotional resilience.

5. Wellness Check-in:

Activity: Schedule regular wellness check-ins to assess your physical and mental well-being.
Rationale: Prioritizing health ensures sustained energy and motivation.
Example:
Frequency: Bi-weekly wellness assessments.
Check-in Elements:
Sleep quality and duration.
Physical activity levels.
Emotional well-being.

Outcome: Insights into areas needing attention and potential adjustments.

6. Work-Life Integration Audit:

Activity: Assess the integration of work and personal life. Identify areas that may need adjustment for better balance.

Rationale: A balanced life prevents burnout and maintains a holistic approach to motivation.

Example:

Audit Elements:

Time allocation for work and personal activities.

Quality of relationships.

Personal growth pursuits.

Outcome: Improved work-life harmony and reduced risk of burnout.

Inspirational Insight:

Example: Consider the routine of Richard Branson, who incorporates daily moments of reflection and physical activity into his schedule. This maintenance routine contributes to Branson's sustained motivation and innovative thinking.

Real-world Example:

The routine of Michelle Obama includes regular physical exercise, mindfulness practices, and intentional moments for family. This comprehensive approach to well-being reflects her commitment to maintaining motivation while navigating a demanding public life.

By integrating these activities into your routine, you create a maintenance plan tailored to sustain motivation over the long term. The examples of successful individuals like Richard Branson and Michelle Obama emphasize the transformative impact of consistent self-care and goal alignment.

This maintenance routine becomes a compass guiding you through the complexities of life, ensuring that your motivation remains resilient and enduring, propelling you toward sustained success.

Self-Motivation Strategies

In the solitary realm of self-motivation, where external stimuli may be scarce, the ability to ignite and sustain one's own fire becomes paramount. This chapter explores powerful techniques for self-motivation, delves into the art of building a resilient mindset, and provides a detailed action plan to create a personalized self-motivation toolkit. Through stories, examples, and actionable insights, we embark on a journey to cultivate the inner strength that propels individuals toward their aspirations, independent of external influences.

Techniques for Motivating Oneself Without External Stimuli:

Self-motivation is an art, and the techniques employed vary from person to person. Consider the story of Eleanor Roosevelt, a figure who navigated challenges with remarkable self-motivation. In the face of adversity, Roosevelt tapped into her inner reservoir of determination and courage. Techniques for self-motivation often involve harnessing internal resources, such as passion, purpose, and self-discipline.

Techniques for Self-Motivation:

- ✓ Intrinsic Goal Alignment: Connect daily tasks with larger, intrinsic goals. This alignment infuses mundane activities with purpose and motivation.
- ✓ Visualization and Affirmations: Engage in daily visualization of success and repeat affirmations that reinforce positive beliefs. This technique shapes a positive mindset.

- ✓ Self-Encouragement: Develop a habit of self-encouragement, acknowledging achievements and progress, no matter how small.

Building a Resilient Mindset:
Resilience is the bedrock of self-motivation. Stories of individuals who faced adversity and emerged stronger showcase the transformative power of a resilient mindset. Malala Yousafzai, the Nobel laureate and advocate for education, exemplifies resilience in the face of adversity. Shot by the Taliban for pursuing education, Malala's resilient mindset fueled her commitment to education rights.
Strategies for Building Resilience:

- ✓ Mindfulness Practices: Incorporate mindfulness techniques to stay present and navigate challenges with clarity and composure.
- ✓ Learning from Setbacks: Embrace setbacks as opportunities for learning and growth. Analyze challenges objectively, extracting lessons for future endeavors.
- ✓ Positive Self-Talk: Cultivate a habit of positive self-talk. Replace self-criticism with constructive and encouraging inner dialogue.

Action Plan: Create a Personalized Self-Motivation Toolkit:
Identify Intrinsic Goals:

- ✓ *Activity:* Reflect on long-term intrinsic goals that fuel your passion.
- ✓ *Outcome:* A list of goals that serve as the core motivation for your endeavors.

Visualization and Affirmation Practice:

- ✓ *Activity:* Dedicate 10 minutes daily to visualize success and repeat positive affirmations.
- ✓ *Outcome:* Enhanced mental clarity, strengthened belief in your abilities.

Self-Encouragement Journal:

- ✓ *Activity:* Maintain a self-encouragement journal. Record achievements, progress, and moments of resilience.
- ✓ *Outcome:* A tangible reminder of your strengths and accomplishments.

Mindfulness Routine:

- ✓ *Activity:* Integrate mindfulness practices, such as meditation or deep breathing, into your daily routine.
- ✓ *Outcome:* Improved focus, reduced stress, and heightened resilience.

Setback Analysis Exercise:

- ✓ *Activity:* When faced with a setback, objectively analyze the situation, identifying lessons for future improvement.
- ✓ *Outcome:* Enhanced adaptability and a proactive approach to challenges.

Positive Self-Talk Commitment:

- ✓ *Activity:* Consciously shift negative self-talk to positive affirmations. Make a commitment to replace self-criticism with self-encouragement.
- ✓ *Outcome:* Cultivation of a positive mindset, reinforcing self-belief.

Inspirational Insight:

Consider the journey of Stephen Hawking, the renowned physicist. Despite facing physical challenges, Hawking's self-motivation stemmed from a passion for unraveling the mysteries of the universe. His resilience and commitment to his work showcase the transformative power of intrinsic motivation.

Real-world Example:

Elon Musk, known for his ambitious ventures like SpaceX and Tesla, relies on a strong self-motivation toolkit. Musk combines goal alignment, visualization, and a resilient mindset to navigate the complexities of entrepreneurship and innovation.

Conclusion:

As you delve into the realm of self-motivation, remember that the strategies and techniques explored in this chapter are tools to be personalized. The stories of Eleanor Roosevelt, Malala Yousafzai, Stephen Hawking, and Elon Musk serve as reminders that the journey of self-motivation is unique for each individual. By crafting your personalized self-motivation toolkit, you embark on a journey of inner strength and determination, paving the way for sustained success and fulfillment.

Creating a Personalized Self-Motivation Toolkit- Action Plan

Objective: Develop a customized set of strategies and practices to ignite and sustain self-motivation, fostering a resilient mindset.

1. Identify Intrinsic Goals:
   - ✓ *Activity:* Reflect on long-term intrinsic goals that fuel your passion.
   - ✓ *Outcome:* A list of goals that serve as the core motivation for your endeavors.

     Example:
   - ✓ Intrinsic Goal: Establish a sustainable business that aligns with personal values.
   - ✓ Passion Connection: The goal aligns with a deep passion for environmental sustainability and ethical business practices.
2. Visualization and Affirmation Practice:
   - ✓ *Activity:* Dedicate 10 minutes daily to visualize success and repeat positive affirmations.
   - ✓ *Outcome:* Enhanced mental clarity, strengthened belief in your abilities.

     Example:
   - ✓ Visualization: Imagine successfully delivering a compelling presentation to stakeholders.
   - ✓ Affirmation: "I am confident and articulate. My ideas have value and resonate with others."
3. Self-Encouragement Journal:
   - ✓ *Activity:* Maintain a self-encouragement journal. Record achievements, progress, and moments of resilience.
   - ✓ *Outcome:* A tangible reminder of your strengths and accomplishments.

     Example:

- ✓ Entry: "Overcame a challenging meeting today by expressing my ideas clearly. Proud of my resilience and ability to navigate difficult situations."

4. Mindfulness Routine:
   - ✓ *Activity:* Integrate mindfulness practices, such as meditation or deep breathing, into your daily routine.
   - ✓ *Outcome:* Improved focus, reduced stress, and heightened resilience.
     Example:
   - ✓ Mindfulness Technique: Five minutes of deep breathing in the morning.
   - ✓ Observation: Increased awareness of thoughts and emotions, leading to a more centered and focused start to the day.
5. Setback Analysis Exercise:
   - ✓ *Activity:* When faced with a setback, objectively analyze the situation, identifying lessons for future improvement.
   - ✓ *Outcome:* Enhanced adaptability and a proactive approach to challenges.
     Example:
   - ✓ Setback: Project deadline extension.
   - ✓ Analysis: Identified areas for better time management and proactive communication. Set a plan to improve these aspects in future projects.
6. Positive Self-Talk Commitment:
   - ✓ *Activity:* Consciously shift negative self-talk to positive affirmations. Make a commitment to replace self-criticism with self-encouragement.
   - ✓ *Outcome:* Cultivation of a positive mindset, reinforcing self-belief.
     Example:

- ✓ Negative Thought: "I'm not good enough for this opportunity."
- ✓ Positive Affirmation: "I have unique skills and experiences that make me well-suited for this challenge. I am capable and resilient."

Inspirational Insight:

Example: Consider the story of Maya Angelou, the acclaimed poet and author. Angelou's self-motivation toolkit included daily affirmations and a commitment to lifelong learning, enabling her to overcome personal challenges and achieve extraordinary success.

Real-world Example:

Michelle Obama's self-motivation toolkit involves daily practices of gratitude, reflection, and goal-setting. These personalized strategies contribute to her resilience and ability to stay motivated in the face of complex challenges.

Your self-motivation toolkit is a dynamic and personal collection of practices that resonate with your unique strengths and aspirations. As you implement this action plan, remember that it's a living document — adjust and refine it as needed. The examples provided are mere starting points; feel free to adapt and tailor each component to align seamlessly with your journey toward sustained self-motivation and fulfillment.

Skills for Motivating Employees

In the intricate tapestry of organizational dynamics, the art of motivating employees is both a science and an empathetic practice. This chapter unravels leadership strategies for inspiring teams, explores the intricacies of employee engagement and performance enhancement, and offers a comprehensive action plan to implement team-building activities in the workplace. By weaving together examples, stories, and actionable insights, we delve into the heart of effective leadership and employee motivation.

Leadership Strategies for Motivating Teams:
Leadership is the cornerstone of employee motivation. The story of Steve Jobs, co-founder of Apple Inc., serves as a testament to visionary leadership. Jobs' ability to inspire innovation and passion among his team members resulted in revolutionary products. Effective leadership strategies include:

- ✓ Visionary Communication: Articulate a compelling vision that resonates with the team's values and aspirations. Jobs' famous product launches were not just presentations; they were showcases of a future he believed in.
- ✓ Empowerment and Autonomy: Delegate responsibilities and empower team members to make decisions. Autonomy fosters a sense of ownership and motivation. Google's 20% time, where employees could pursue passion projects, exemplifies this strategy.

- ✓ Recognition and Appreciation: Acknowledge and appreciate individual and team achievements. Public recognition, as seen in the "employee of the month" tradition, creates a positive and motivating work environment.

Employee Engagement and Performance Enhancement:

Engaged employees are motivated employees. The narrative of Zappos, an online shoe and clothing retailer, revolves around a unique company culture that prioritizes employee happiness. Strategies for enhancing employee engagement and performance include:

- ✓ Purposeful Work: Connect employees to the larger purpose of their work. Zappos, for instance, aligns its employees with the mission of delivering happiness through exceptional customer service.
- ✓ Continuous Learning and Development: Provide opportunities for skill enhancement and career growth. LinkedIn's "InDay" allows employees to dedicate a day to learning and innovation, fostering a culture of continuous improvement.
- ✓ Feedback and Performance Reviews: Establish regular feedback mechanisms and performance reviews. Constructive feedback and goal-setting sessions contribute to employee development and motivation.

Action Plan: Implement Team-Building Activities in the Workplace:

Identify Team Dynamics:

- ✓ *Activity:* Assess team dynamics and identify areas for improvement.
- ✓ *Outcome:* Understanding team strengths and weaknesses lays the foundation for targeted team-building activities.

Customize Team-Building Activities:

- ✓ *Activity:* Tailor team-building activities based on identified needs. Consider activities like problem-solving challenges or collaborative projects.
- ✓ *Outcome:* Customized activities enhance specific teamwork skills and foster a sense of camaraderie.

Facilitate Open Communication:

- ✓ *Activity:* Schedule regular team meetings to encourage open communication. Implement strategies like roundtable discussions or brainstorming sessions.
- ✓ *Outcome:* Improved communication promotes trust and collaboration among team members.

Incorporate Fun and Socialization:

- ✓ *Activity:* Integrate fun and socializing into the work environment. This could include team lunches, game nights, or themed events.
- ✓ *Outcome:* A positive and enjoyable workplace contributes to increased team morale and motivation.

Celebrate Milestones and Achievements:

- ✓ *Activity:* Acknowledge and celebrate team milestones and achievements. This could involve recognition ceremonies or team outings.
- ✓ *Outcome:* Celebrating successes reinforces a sense of accomplishment and motivates the team to pursue future goals.

Inspirational Insight:

Example: The success story of Pixar Animation Studios under the leadership of Ed Catmull and John Lasseter showcases the power of collaborative creativity. Regular "Braintrust" meetings, where directors provided candid feedback, fostered a culture of collaboration and innovation.

Real-world Example:

The employee-centric approach of Salesforce, a cloud-based software company, is evident in its "Ohana" culture. Regular team-building events, volunteer activities, and a focus on employee well-being contribute to a motivated and engaged workforce.

Effective leadership and employee motivation are symbiotic. As you implement team-building activities, remember that each team is unique, and the success of these activities lies in their alignment with team dynamics and goals. The stories of Steve Jobs, Zappos, Pixar, and Salesforce illustrate that a motivated team is not just productive; it is innovative, resilient, and capable of achieving remarkable success. This chapter invites leaders to embrace the role of motivator-in-chief, fostering an environment where teams thrive and individuals find purpose and fulfillment in their work.

Implementing Team-Building Activities in the Workplace: Action Plan

Objective: Foster a positive and collaborative work environment through targeted team-building activities. Strengthen team dynamics, improve communication, and enhance morale.

1. Identify Team Dynamics:

- ✓ *Activity:* Conduct a team assessment to identify strengths, weaknesses, and areas for improvement.
- ✓ *Outcome:* Understanding team dynamics provides insights into the specific aspects that need attention during team-building activities.

  Example:
- ✓ Assessment Tools: Surveys, interviews, or facilitated discussions.
- ✓ Identified Dynamics: Communication gaps, lack of trust in decision-making, and limited collaboration on projects.

2. Customize Team-Building Activities:

- ✓ *Activity:* Tailor team-building activities based on identified needs. Consider activities that address communication, trust-building, or collaborative problem-solving.
- ✓ *Outcome:* Customized activities enhance specific teamwork skills and foster a sense of camaraderie.

  Example:
- ✓ Activity 1: Team-building workshop focused on effective communication and active listening.

- ✓ Activity 2: Collaborative project or escape room challenge to encourage problem-solving and teamwork.

3. **Facilitate Open Communication:**
   - ✓ *Activity:* Schedule regular team meetings to encourage open communication. Implement strategies like roundtable discussions or brainstorming sessions.
   - ✓ *Outcome:* Improved communication promotes trust and collaboration among team members.

     Example:
   - ✓ Meeting Format: Monthly roundtable discussions where team members share updates, challenges, and ideas.
   - ✓ Outcome: Increased transparency, understanding, and a sense of shared purpose.
4. **Incorporate Fun and Socialization:**
   - ✓ *Activity:* Integrate fun and socializing into the work environment. This could include team lunches, game nights, or themed events.
   - ✓ *Outcome:* A positive and enjoyable workplace contributes to increased team morale and motivation.

     Example:
   - ✓ Activity: Monthly team lunches or virtual happy hours.
   - ✓ Outcome: Strengthened team bonds, improved morale, and a more enjoyable work atmosphere.
5. Celebrate Milestones and Achievements:
   - ✓ *Activity:* Acknowledge and celebrate team milestones and achievements. This could involve recognition ceremonies or team outings.

- ✓ *Outcome:* Celebrating successes reinforces a sense of accomplishment and motivates the team to pursue future goals.
- ✓ *Example:*
- ✓ Recognition Ceremony: Quarterly awards for outstanding team contributions.
- ✓ Outcome: Increased motivation, a sense of pride, and a positive team culture.

Implementation Timeline:

Month	Activity
1	Team dynamics assessment and initial feedback session.
2	Customized team-building workshop addressing identified needs.
3	Monthly roundtable discussions to foster open communication.
4	Fun and socialization event (e.g., team lunch or game night).
5	Recognition ceremony for achievements and milestones.
6+	Rotate activities based on ongoing assessments and team feedback.

Monitoring and Adjustments:

Regularly assess the impact of team-building activities through feedback sessions and follow-up surveys. Adjust the plan based on evolving team dynamics and emerging needs.

Inspirational Insight:

Example: The success of Google's "Project Aristotle," which aimed to understand effective team dynamics, emphasizes the importance of psychological safety and clear communication in building successful teams.

Real-world Example:

Salesforce's "Ohana" culture includes regular team-building activities such as volunteer events and themed celebrations. This approach contributes to a positive and collaborative work environment.

By implementing this action plan, you lay the foundation for a workplace where individuals feel connected, motivated, and engaged. Remember that the success of team-building activities lies in their alignment with the unique needs and dynamics of your team. As you navigate this journey, celebrate the progress, learn from the experiences, and adapt the plan to create a workplace where collaboration thrives, and each team member feels valued and motivated.

Conclusion:
Igniting the Flames of Motivation

As we conclude this journey through the realms of motivation and success, it's essential to reflect on the profound insights and actionable strategies we've explored together. The fabric of motivation is woven with threads of inspiration, resilience, and purpose. Let's distill the essence of our exploration into key takeaways that can illuminate your path toward personal and professional success.

Key Takeaways:

- ✓ Motivation is Intrinsic: At its core, motivation springs from within. It's not a fleeting external force but a flame that can be kindled and sustained by aligning with your values, passions, and goals.
- ✓ Leadership Fuels Motivation: Whether leading oneself or a team, effective leadership is instrumental in fostering motivation. Visionary communication, empowerment, and recognition are potent tools in a leader's arsenal.
- ✓ Continuous Improvement: The journey toward sustained motivation is a continuous process of improvement. Regular assessments, feedback loops, and adaptable strategies ensure ongoing growth and resilience.
- ✓ Team Collaboration is Vital: In workplaces, the synergy of motivated individuals forms the backbone of success. Team-building activities, open communication, and a culture of

celebration contribute to a motivated and engaged workforce.

- ✓ Self-Motivation is a Skill: Equipping yourself with the tools for self-motivation is a skill that can be honed. Visualization, affirmations, and a commitment to resilience pave the way for individual triumphs.

Application of Principles:

Now armed with these insights, the onus lies on you, the reader, to breathe life into these principles. Consider the story of J.K. Rowling, who, fueled by her intrinsic motivation, transformed rejection into the wizarding world of Harry Potter. Apply the strategies discussed in each chapter, tailoring them to your unique circumstances and aspirations.

As you navigate the intricate dance of motivation, remember the lessons from leaders like Elon Musk, who, through a personalized self-motivation toolkit, reshaped industries. Apply visionary communication in your leadership, empower those around you, and cultivate resilience.

In the workplace, emulate Salesforce's "Ohana" culture by implementing team-building activities. Just as Pixar's collaborative creativity thrived in the "Braintrust" meetings, create spaces for open communication and idea exchange.

Resources for Further Exploration:

The journey doesn't end here. To deepen your understanding and refine your approach to motivation, consider exploring the following various resources. The internet is full of them- books, courses and workshops.

Networking:
Engage with mentors, peers, and communities dedicated to personal and professional development. Learn from the experiences and insights of others.

Final Words:
In the grand tapestry of life, motivation is the vibrant thread that weaves dreams into reality. As you take these principles and apply them to your journey, remember the words of Maya Angelou: "You may not control all the events that happen to you, but you can decide not to be reduced by them." Embrace the challenges, celebrate the victories, and let the flame of motivation illuminate your path to enduring success.

May your endeavors be fueled by passion, guided by purpose, and sustained by the unwavering belief that within you lies the power to achieve greatness. This is not just a conclusion; it's an invitation to embark on a life illuminated by the brilliance of your own motivation.

About the Author
'GERARD ASSEY'

Gerard Assey is a Graduate in Economics, a PGD in Management (HRD) and holds a Doctorate in Leadership. Gerard holds several International Qualifications in Sales, Debt Collection, Training & Teaching, and is a 'Fellow' of the prestigious 'Institute of Sales & Marketing Management'-UK, a Certified NLP Practitioner, a 'Certified Trainer', an 'Accredited Management Teacher-Behavioral Sciences', a 'Certified Competency Facilitator', a 'Certified Management Consultant'- (the International credentials of a professional management consultant, awarded in accordance with global standards of the ICMCI); and a Certification from the University of Michigan in 'Successful Negotiation: Essential Strategies and Skills'

He is also a Member of the 'National Association of Sales Professionals' backed with several years experience in varied industries, both in India and Overseas. He also holds an 'Etiquette Consultant' Certification from the USA (by Sue Fox, Author of Best Seller: 'Business Etiquette for Dummies'. She has trained some of the top celebrities' world over). He was also a recipient of a scholarship for extensive training in Japan on 'Corporate Management for India'.

Gerard Assey is 'Founder & Chief Corporate Trainer' of the Group: **'Citius, Altius, Fortius Unlimited'**- an organization that **celebrated 20 years of Glorious Service** in 2021, focusing on 3 Core Competencies:

People. Performance. Profit; in functional areas of Sales & Marketing, HR & Organizational Development, covering Recruitment, Training & Consultancy!

Having managed organizations with large Sales Forces in India & Overseas, his specialization cover extensive areas of Sales Training (All levels - Presentation, Negotiation, Key/ Strategic Accounts Management & Managerial Skills for all sectors), Bid Proposal/ Capture Planning/ Management Trainings, Retail Sales, Customer Service & Customer Retention Programs, Training for Prevention & Collection of Debt, Self & Personal Development Programs (Time Management, Teamwork & Team Building, Business Etiquette & Personal Grooming, Leadership & Managerial Skills, People Management Skills, Train-the-Trainer etc), including preparation of Custom-designed Business Manuals for Internal (HR, Induction, and Sales etc) & External use (Instruction, User Manuals).

Gerard has successfully conducted over 6150 Trainings & Workshops (as of April '24) all across India, Middle East, Africa, Europe & S.E. Asia. Besides public programs conducted regularly, both in India & Overseas, he has some of the top names as clients whom he services from Single Owners to large Public & Government undertakings, covering all sectors, for their in-house needs.

His website: www.CollectionSkills.com is the only one in this part of the world to be featured in the 'Collections & Credit Risk Magazine-USA' under 'Who's Who in Training' and ranks TOP, along with other websites listed below on most search engines.

Gerard is author of 120 books already (April 2024)

A few of our business related books:

1. Bite-sized Bits on Commonsense Management
2. Heart to Heart on Life's Principles'
3. How to become a Successful Manager
4. The Sales Professionals' Master Workbook of S.Y.S.T.E.M.S
5. The Professional Business Email Etiquette Handbook & Guide
6. The Professional Business Video-Conferencing Etiquette Handbook & Guide
7. Professional Presentation Skills
8. Exceptional Customer Service
9. Professional Tele-Marketing Skills
10. Professional Debt Collection Skills
11. The G.R.E.A.T. Sales & Service Workbook
12. Sales Training Advantage for Results (*The Ultimate Sales Training Manual to enable you stand out as a S.T.A.R.*)
13. CEO Daily Planner & Organizer
14. The Sales Professionals' Master Daily Planner
15. The Professional Debt Collector's Master Daily Planner
16. My Daily Planner & Organizer
17. MY EMERGENCY INFORMATION RECORD (Family Emergency & Peace of Mind Planner)
18. The Ultimate Therapist & Counselors Planner and Organizer
19. Building an Ethical Workplace
20. Managing Relationships at Work
21. Managing Business Meetings Effectively
22. Effective Delegation Skills
23. Goal Setting for Success
24. B2B Selling by Email
25. Professional Business Etiquette & Grooming
26. Dining Etiquette & Table Manners
27. Effective Networking Skills
28. Grooming, Etiquette & Manners for Teens, Young Adults & Future Leaders
29. Inter-Personal Skills
30. Get Ready, Get Hired!
31. Selling in a Recession
32. Effective Receivables Management in an Economic Downturn!
33. Real Estate & Property Sales Training

34. Credit Sales & Accounts Receivable Management
35. Selling Skills for Real Estate & Property Advisors
36. Take G.R.E.A.T. C.A.R.E!
37. Spa, Salon & Health Club Selling Skills
38. Selling Travel, Holiday & MICE Services
39. Selling Skills for Spa's, Salons & Health Clubs
40. Retailing in Salons & Spas
41. Selling Holiday, Vacation, Tours & Packages
42. The Power of Sales Referrals
43. Selling Luxury
44. Technical Selling Skills
45. Financial Advisors Sales Training
46. Dealing with Burnout at Work Monopolize Your Markets
47. Selling to Affluent Customers
48. Growing up with Grace
49. Financial Selling Skills
50. *The Effective Manager's Guide: Key Skills to Thrive*
51. From Aspiring to Inspiring: A Guide for New Managers on the Rise
52. The Power of Focus
53. Selling with Integrity: Sell Like Jesus The Perfect Role Model!
54. 31 Habits of Champions: Your 31-Day Journey to Greatness
55. Rejecting Grasshopper Talk: From Grasshopper to Giant-Killer-*Defeating Giants Daily!*
56. Navigate the AI-Powered Future of Bid & Proposals: Up-Skill to Stay Relevant with Alternative Career Paths & Opportunities
57. Hiring Sales Winners
58. Present with Impact
59. Success Unlocked: *Breaking Free from Habits that Hold You Back*
60. Complaints to Cheers, Feedback to Gold: Mastering Complaints Management
61. Thriving Together: *Cultivating Diversity, Equity, and Inclusion*
62. Coaching Skills for Sales Managers
63. Soaring to Success in Business & Leadership: Swifter, Higher, Stronger!
64. From Classroom to Podium: A Student's Guide to Powerful Public Speaking & Presentation Skills

65. Developing Self-Discipline
66. The CEO's 31-Day Power Plan: Unlocking Success through Essential Traits
67. Credibility Matters
68. A Winning Attitude
69. Bid & Proposal Management Using AI
70. Sales Forecasting: A Practical & Proven Guide to Strategic Sales Forecasting
71. Elevate & Energize: *50 Dynamic & Fun Activities for Peak Workplace Morale*
72. 'Sales SOS! Sales on Fire! *30 Days to Conquer Chaos & the Nightmares of Success!'*
73. Mastering Sales Managerial Skills: *Building High-Performing Teams & Driving Exceptional Results*
74. Eagle-Eyed Leadership: Unleashing the Power of 31 Lessons from Eagles
75. The Ultimate Employee Training Guide: *Training Today, Leading Tomorrow*
76. Being More Accountable at Work
77. Creating a Culture of Continuous Improvement
78. Effective Questioning & Listening Skills
79. The Power of Value Selling
80. The Growth Mindset
81. Mastering Professional Help Desk Skills
82. The Power to Lead with Empathy
83. Being Prepared: The Key to Unlocking Success
84. Youthful Spark-Youth Energizers, Activities and Games-Igniting the Fun in Youth
85. Ignite your Motivation for Success

Besides regularly contributing to business & trade journals, including international ones such as the 'Creative Training Techniques' and the 'Sales News' of the U.S.A, He is also a member of several prestigious bodies & trade associations, having participated in many Conferences & Workshops in India & Overseas.

Prior to his last assignment of leading & managing a large MNC as head, Gerard had a 3-year stint in the Middle East as a Consultant with a leading British Consultancy Firm.

As the past 'Official Country Representative' for the International Business Award- 'THE STEVIES'-(the business world's own Oscar) for about 4 years- he ensured a few Indian companies that qualify for the same every year!

Gerard can be contacted at:
Email: training@Sales-Training.in,training@CollectionSkills.com
Websites:

www.Sales-Training.in
www.EtiquetteWorks.in
www.CollectionSkills.com
www.RetailSalesTraining.in
www.SalesTrainingIndia.com
www.ManualPreparation.com
www.TrainingWithPuppets.com
www.FirstContactAcademy.com
www.SalesAndMarketingRecruiter.com

Our TRAININGS that can help your team

- ✓ **Sales Effectiveness**: Selling Skills for any Sector: Service/ Logistics/ FMCG Realty/ Insurance & Finance/ Media/ SPA's, Health Clubs & Salons/ Key Account Management, Effective Negotiation Skills/ Bid & Proposal Management Skills/ Retail Sales Training: Any Sector (Auto, Jewelry, Clothing, Luxury etc)
- ✓ **Customer Service Skills**-Complaints Handling & Customer Retention
- ✓ **Debt Prevention & Collection Skills**
- ✓ **Etiquette & Grooming**
- ✓ **Leadership & Managerial Skills**
- ✓ **Self & Personal Development Skills**: Presentation Skills/ Effective Communication Skills/Business Proposal Writing Skills/ Problem Solving & Decision Making Skills/ Empowering Secretaries-The perfect PA! (For Secretaries & PA's)/ Effective Time Management/ Teamwork & Teambuilding/ P.R.I.D.E- **P**ersonal **R**esponsibility **I**n **D**elivering **E**xcellence

www.ingramcontent.com/pod-product-compliance
Lightning Source LLC
LaVergne TN
LVHW010113170826
845678LV00012B/2393

* 9 7 8 8 1 9 7 1 1 2 1 6 4 *